heal this
2—

365 Days of Scrambled Eggs

LIFE AFTER A MASSIVE STROKE AND HOW TO KEEP LAUGHING

By Barb Kwaiser
with Bruce Kwaiser
and Linda Worrell

Illustrations by Kris Wynne

ISBN: 9798834285588
ASIN: B0B57DCNCJ

Cover design by: Izabela Design
Illustrations by: Kris Wynne

Library of Congress Control Number: in process
Printed in the United States of America

CONTENTS

Dedicated to all the "Pearls" in our lives.

Alison Starkey PT MBA MHA CAPS CDP CFPS
Owner, Gaitway of Charlotte LLC, Charlotte NC

*"I have never had a client who tried as
hard or achieved such outcomes."*

Stroke can be a devastating phenomenon. However, no two strokes are the same as no two brains are the same. We are all wired differently depending on our life experience.

A bleed causes stroke out of a diseased artery or a clot in a brain artery. Each method of attack blocks oxygen to the brain, and the brain ahead of the blockage or bleeding dies. The degree of disability depends on the specific location and severity of the brain affected. Even two strokes in the same location can have very different levels of disability.

The goal of therapy after a stroke is to recruit another part of the brain, to do what the now dead brain used to do, a process called "neuroplasticity." Recovery requires practice, repetition, and facilitation to create new brain pathways that become automatic and result in recovery of function and a semblance to return to everyday life.

Consider an able person learning the piano. The first lesson is difficult and frustrating as your hands adapt to a new skill. However, with practice, those notes become easier to find and execute. With significant training, encouragement, and practice, creating notes on the keyboard becomes automatic and rewarding. This process is a version of "brain training" and is the basis of neurological recovery and rehabilitation for stroke victims.

Therapists follow neurological concepts familiar to parents watching their babies learn and grow. At first, they are helpless little bundles that need complete care. Then, as they practice rolling, sitting up, and eventually standing, they build new pathways they will use for the rest of their life. It is those pathways that we sequence with neurological rehab. The adage is true – you did have to roll, sit, and stand before you could walk and run. An experienced therapist facilitates this sequence of skills, resulting in the best possible outcomes.

There are several "intangibles" that really help recovery. First, having a positive mindset has been proven time and time again to be the most valuable asset in stroke recovery. Patients who "give up" are simply unable to form the new pathways and suffer a higher level of disability.

In Barb's case, she got her positive attitude rolling right out of the gate. Her infectious humor brought her through the challenging initial stages. Studies also show that having a supportive family is very indicative of a better outcome. Bruce Kwaiser was brilliant at keeping Barb's motivation going while dealing with his own healthcare challenges.

There is a lot I can say about the Kwaisers – but know this. I have been a physical therapist for over 35 years. I have never had a client who tried as hard or achieved such outcomes with a genuine level of grit and determination with a loving husband to cheer her at every stage. I do not call other past patients to hear their voices, but I check in on the Kwaisers and love to hear about their latest news.

I admire Barb's tenacity, Bruce's love and support, and their amazing marriage. What a couple these two are. What an honor to know them!

Enjoy reading their story.

— *Alison Starkey*

Allow Me to Introduce the Kwaisers

I have had the good fortune to know Barb and Bruce Kwaiser for several years, but it was not until Barb suffered a massive stroke that I really got to know them.

Barb and Bruce spent precious hours with me, reliving and telling the story of their experience as they look back on the 18 months of enduring the most horrific scare the couple could have imagined.

According to the Centers for Disease Control and Prevention (CDC), more than 795,000 people in the United States have a stroke annually, and 80% are preventable. This reality makes it even more inspiring to learn about the grit and good humor the couple brought to their challenge. They have looked back at the painful, scary, positive, and even joyful parts of their experience and hope others can learn and benefit.

If I have honored them well, you will come to know Barb as endlessly optimistic with a wicked sense of humor and Bruce as hard driving with a heart bigger than most full-time caregivers wearing a bra. (Barb inspired me to say that.) We hope you also enjoy the original artwork from their loving daughter Kris, which accompanies Barb's special tips and quips.

My special thanks to Diane Dean and Stephen Worrell for editing support and to all our prereaders for their thoughtful and caring feedback.

— Linda Worrell, friend, and coauthor

365 Days Of Scrambled Eggs

LIFE AFTER A MASSIVE STROKE AND HOW TO KEEP LAUGHING

DAY 1: BARB

THE NIGHT OF THE PARTY

Looking around my closet, deciding what to wear, I spotted the new spaghetti-strap satin dress I bought for an upcoming wedding. The dress could serve double duty since tonight's guests will not be at the wedding. Pairing the outfit with my metallic heels accentuated the sheen of the dress. While it was perfect, I settled on a more practical sparkly flat, knowing I'd be more comfortable standing. The invite did say "country-club casual," but it's the holidays, so I'm sure most of the girls attending will choose the dressier definition. As for the guys, I knew to check on what Bruce is wearing.

It was December 11, 2020, and we had been invited to join a special evening benefiting St. Jude Hospital, hosted in the home of our good friends Bob & Amor. The event featured an extravagant seven-course meal with wine pairings, prepared by our country club's head chef, Josh, for their eight lucky guests.

I pinched myself, thinking how lucky we were to have these friends, this home, and this lifestyle.

After all the holiday parties we had already attended this December, I realized the dress was a bit snug. Guess it doesn't help I've given up on following the Mediterranean diet Dr. Cook suggested. Maybe I should add some Spanx? Heck, I'll just add a shawl to cover up the roll. For this meal, I put my comfort over looks.

I twirled in my pretty dress over to Bruce's closet and got the big grin and wink I'd hoped for. Lucky me to have had this guy by my side for over 60 years.

Bruce raised his pre-party glass of Crown Royal in a toast. Standing there in his Tommy John briefs and a golf shirt, I gave him the look.

"But these are my best TJs and golf shirt!" said Bruce. I reminded him this was a special dinner and to please select something more appropriate. Knowing there was no point in arguing, Bruce dressed in his church pants, a pressed shirt, and cashmere vest. He finished his drink, and off we went.

Mariah Carey's *All I Want for Christmas Is You* was playing when Amor, our hostess, opened the door to greet us, instantly making us feel special. Bob and Amor's luxurious home on the north shore of Lake Norman looked like Disney's Magic Kingdom with life-sized nutcrackers, multiple Christmas trees, and hundreds of colored lights. Seeing me study the decorations, Amor explained the grandkids were coming for Christmas. It reminded me of the Big Red Boat cruise we took in 1999 with our kids and grands, just before Bruce retired from Dow Chemical after 34 years.

I set my purse down and accepted the champagne a waiter handed me. Then, knowing I'd be having more than a few drinks, I figured I better commit to memory where I placed my purse. It was no surprise the other women looked stunning. Even the guys looked great. What an added pleasure to be mask free, although I did note the waiter and other staff were masked. We had been assured all attending had received their COVID vaccines, and we were asked to take our temperature and stay home if we showed any symptoms.

Nine months into the pandemic, we were careful about masking, hand washing, and following all the CDC recommendations. Even more so when Bruce was diagnosed with prostate cancer five months earlier. Our world had been turned upside down ever since, researching treatment options, getting second opinions, etc.

We were set to stay in Atlanta, beginning January 3, for his treatment, so the last thing we needed was for either of us to get COVID. Seeming to reassure me, Bruce squeezed my shoulder, winked at me, and said, "Don't worry. No bug will survive this evening of drinking."

Amor invited us to find our place cards as the cocktail hour segued to dinner. It felt special to be put next to her at the table.

Pine boughs and candles filled the room with the scent of Christmas, and the silver and gold place settings twinkled in the chandelier's reflection. This will be an excellent evening to forget about Bruce's health news and party like before, I decided.

Our host, Bob, stood at the other end of the table and shared thanks for helping them support St. Jude and asked us to bow our heads in prayer. At its conclusion, all eight guests joined in, saying, "Amen."

Bruce led the way by raising his glass to our hosts, and we all joined in. The music pumped back up over the speakers with *Santa Baby* playing. No surprise who began the sing-along.

Chef Josh and the servers cut short the revelry, arriving with our first course of seared scallops with siracha bacon. Josh explained the ingredients, his preparation, and the Gewurztraminer wine being poured to pair with the beautifully arranged dish.

Between bites, I heard how Cathy and Jim, seated across from us, would be spending their Christmas. On my other side, Bruce and the others were listening to John tell his favorite joke for the 38th time. A master storyteller, they were all laughing and encouraging him.

As we all chatted non-stop, more courses were presented: lobster, roasted duck, and beef tenderloin with foie gras butter. The preparation for each dish was described, although the attention paid was diminishing along with each different fine wine poured.

My waistline was expanding with each course, and I congratulated myself on my good judgment not to wear shapewear.

The finale was a decadent seven-layer chocolate cake. After the dishes were cleared, folks lingered at the table finishing half-empty bottles, still telling stories, and singing along with the music. Amor and I talked, but I have no idea what we discussed, except that I told her I needed to use the restroom and asked which one I should use.

This is the part of the story the book title warned you about.

Bruce thought he heard me say I had to use the restroom and wondered if I was subtly asking for help to get up. As I suddenly rested my head on his shouldered, he whispered, "Barb, Honey?"

When there was no response from me, and my head didn't budge, he said to me again, "Barb, hey Barbie!"

Bruce remembers nervous laughter from others at the

table, followed by gasps.

Bruce tells me Cathy jumped up from across the table and said, "Barb, hey Barb, can you hear me?" Then, she ran around to my side.

Enter my first guardian angel.

It is my great fortune that Cathy is not only a trusted friend, but also a registered nurse. She noticed I'd just spoken to Amor with slurred words and a drooping mouth. She told Bruce, "I think Barb is stroking. We need to call 911 now!"

Bruce has a hazy recollection of someone from the far end of the table saying, "Don't call the paramedics; they'll see all the wine bottles and just think she's drunk!" It was obvious they hadn't realized how serious the situation was.

Cathy ordered her husband, "Jim, call 911 NOW! Barb is having a stroke."

I remember Cathy comforting me. Her hands were on my shoulders, telling me to breathe through my nose and blow out through my mouth. Just let go, I remember thinking, others will take care of you now.

Bruce saw Jim pull out his phone and dial, and Joyce clasp her hands and whisper a prayer. He says he felt his adrenalin rise and his heart sink simultaneously.

Mr. Stroke had obviously shown up.

I was fortunate the ambulance was close, as the local EMT's arrived within 5 minutes. Unfortunately, I have no awareness of this time, yet I'm certain Cathy would have been involved, telling the EMT's what she observed.

Bruce also has no recollection of how I was assessed or moved from our dining table to the exit across the room. "Can you believe this is a total blank for me?" Bruce says today, hanging his head and shaking it, "But I finally snapped to attention." He recalls thinking, when they loaded me onto a gurney and out the door, "I needed to figure out if I am riding along, or driving my car, and where the heck they are taking my Barb."

I have a weird cloudy memory of thinking, wait, where's my purse? Shouldn't someone be giving it to me if I'm leaving? Maybe it was being jostled around by the EMT's that triggered my scrambled brain.

Bruce tells me this was when he dialed Dr. Cook on his phone. This doesn't surprise me because Bruce is a take-charge kind of guy, but also because Dr. Cook is our primary physician that we both have used and trusted for 30 years. Since Bruce was worried the EMT might take me to the nearest small regional hospital, he needed Dr. Cook's advice. So, can you believe Dr. Cook answered on the second ring at nearly 10 p.m. on a Friday?

I'm sure they were both all business, and Dr. Cook told

Bruce that for a stroke, we should go to Charlotte Medical Center main campus which has a trauma center. It's what is called CMC Main. Ambulance crews are instructed to go to the nearest emergency care for some conditions, but they agreed to the longer trip. Or maybe it was the look I know Bruce gives when there is no point arguing.

"Everything will be okay, Barb," I think I recall Bruce calling out to me.

Once the ambulance doors were ready to close, Bruce started to head to our car, as they told him to follow rather than ride along.

"Everyone was in complete shock and didn't know what to do next," said Bruce. "But before I could get to my car, Jim said, 'Come on, I'll drive.'" So, Jim, Bob and Bruce all got into Jim's car and got behind the ambulance. They obviously should have been thinking about all they'd had to drink, and maybe that's why Jim offered to drive. Bruce says it seemed to take forever getting to CMC Main.

I was never fully conscious but seem to remember parts of the ambulance ride. I sensed we were going fast, although I don't remember hearing the siren. I recollect that everyone was trying to console me and make me feel safe. The attendants were so busy I didn't think I had to entertain them.

In case you didn't know, riding in an ambulance is like

a noisy roller coaster. You can feel every twist and bump times ten. I remember someone wiping me and cleaning me off, and was later told I had projectile vomited at least five courses of the seven-course meal. At first, they thought I was hemorrhaging but then decided it was the volcano of red wine. What a waste of great food and wine.

Light the lights; the Broadway show "CODE STROKE" opens tonight.

Records show it was nearing 11:00 p.m. when my ambulance arrived, and I was admitted to the ER. The medical team was everywhere, shining enormously bright lights in my eyes and calling out commands. The light was like knives jabbing my eyes and their voices sounded like fuzz. I was trying to make sense of it all, but my brain felt like a jumbled mess. Where was Bruce? Couldn't he help answer their questions?

Before I could muster a single word to answer, they'd ask me something else. Then they moved to the foot of my bed. The doctors must have been rubbing a probe against my bare feet because the medical report says I reacted slightly on my right foot, but there was no response on the left.

The attending doctor confirmed a CODE STROKE diagnosis and had neurology order the life-saving clot-dissolving medicine, TPA (tissue plasminogen activator). It was administered immediately.

They must have changed me out of my soiled dress and into a hospital gown, but I know I was helpless to assist. Someone must have been twisting my wedding bands to remove them because I have this memory that it was me turning my mother's rings like I did when I was a kid, spinning them around and around. It gave me some comfort.

Here comes another light show. I was given a CT scan, which I've had before. But this time, the lights were excruciating. It was like a kaleidoscope of spinning graffiti images all around me. "Calm down, guys!" I wanted to tell the techs and my brain.

Ugh, I vomited again, this time *inside* the CT tunnel. The techs halted the procedure. With my condition getting worse, they needed to intubate me for airway protection. So, a trip back to ER for that procedure.

I had been in Emergency for about 90 minutes when my attending doctor ordered an embolectomy. My abbreviated CT scan had apparently confirmed this was the appropriate next step. For this, I was rolled into the interventional radiology (IR) surgical suite.

I keep reminding myself how fortunate I was to have this top stroke trauma center available to me. I like to imagine it like an episode of "Grey's Anatomy" with their choreographed moves, and the orchestration of removing the carotid and cerebral artery clots my scan had identified.

During a nearly three-hour surgery, the surgeons had to make three passes to clear individual vessels. Finally, the surgeons felt they had removed all the blockage possible without additional risk. Per protocol, I was taken back for CT scans to confirm their work.

I was moved to the Intensive Care Unit in critical but stable condition.

At some point, I don't know when, I woke up with more bright lights and people poking at me. The room was too noisy and chaotic for Heaven, I remember thinking. So, it must mean I'm still alive. God is not ready for me yet.

I hoped Bruce knew this too, but I had no idea where he was, so I repeated the words in my mind that he said to me before the ambulance doors closed, "Everything will be okay."

DAY 1: BRUCE

LIFE CHANGES FAST
THAT'S AN ENORMOUS UNDERSTATEMENT

Jim safely followed the speeding ambulance, and with Bob also along, we arrived at Charlotte Medical Center in Uptown Charlotte around 11:00 p.m. I called Dr. Cook again in route, and I guess he tried to get me to calm down while he promised to stay available and keep me informed.

Jim pulled up to the Emergency entrance as close as he could so I could jump out of the car and run to the door. But a big burly cop quickly looked me up and down, put his hand out, and said, "Nope. Can't come in." The cop was armed, so I stopped cold but explained my wife was being admitted for a stroke. I'm sure I kept trying to negotiate, but he repeated, "No, if you are not the patient, you can't come in," adding, "It's COVID rules, man."

> This is the crazy world we have come to when a guy can't be with his wife when she needs him.

Bob and Jim were behind me by now and caught the last

warning and pulled me back toward the car. We got back in, but I continued staring at the ER door, willing the police to take a break so I could sneak in.

It was well over an hour and a half when, finally, my phone rang with a number I didn't recognize. It was the attending ER doc informing me they had to intubate Barb and were taking her to surgery.

I'll be honest with you; I don't even remember the details of this call, but now medical reports are telling me what was discussed. I do remember Bob suggested we consult with Dr. Cook again. Bob tells me I was white as a sheet, so maybe Bob wanted medical advice on me as much as getting his take on Barb's surgery.

Dr. Cook answered quickly and reassured me of the track record of CMC. He said he would keep tabs on her but reminded me he had limited access and authority in this hospital system.

We sat in that damn cold parking lot for hours. I'm sure Bob and Jim understood I would not leave until I knew if Barb had pulled through. We attempted small talk to pass the hours, starting and stopping the car to stay warm. I hoped my mobile phone battery would hold out, not knowing how long we would be there.

All I could think about was Barb, but the guys wanted to know more about the prostate cancer treatments I was scheduled to get at the Emory Proton Therapy Center in Atlanta starting in January. We had booked an Airbnb for the month and a half it would take to get all 29 treatments. Would that even be possible now?

Dr. Cook called me a couple times as we waited in the car, and at about 1:30 a.m., he told me Barb survived the surgery and was going to Intensive Care. It made me mad then and even more angry now that Dr. Cook, not the hospital, was giving me the news, I needed. This was only the beginning of the frustration I would experience with the medical communities.

He suggested I go home. There was nothing I could do there. Reluctantly, I agreed and told my friends we could leave.

I can scarcely remember the ride home. Did we get my car at Bob's house? Or did they take me directly home? I don't recall, but I remember the dead silence when I walked into our house...alone. After tonight, nothing would be like it was before.

TIP FROM BARB

1

Learn how to recognize a stroke.

Your chances of having a registered nurse with you in the event of a stroke are slim, so learn how to do this yourself.

There are tips in the back of the book to start your education.

TIP FROM BARB

2

Do not hesitate to call 911.

You get a handsome EMT to sweep you off your feet.

TIP FROM BARB

3

You shouldn't have to ask for TPA.

But do it anyway.

The drug, Tissue Plasminogen Activator (TPA) is a powerful agent that dissolves blood clots when administered within the first 3 hours of having a stroke. Time is of the essence. Ask (or have someone ask for you) if you are a candidate.

TIP FROM BARB

4

Have a primary physician you trust like a friend.

The culture of a doctor's practice comes from the top and will reflect on your total patient experience. Let your doctor and his team get to know you and you get to know them.

Consider using the same doctor (or practice) as your spouse. Get your doctor's personal phone number for times of emergency.

BARB'S QUIPS

My response to the doctor shining bright lights in my eyes in the exam room:

Do you know where you are?

"Yes... Hell!"

DAY 2 TO DAY 10: BARB

THE HOSPITAL

On December 12, the day after my massive stroke, all I did was sleep. I'm sure skilled nurses were attentively doing everything for me, looking after the tubes and bandages that appeared overnight.

Bruce tells me he was up at 6 a.m. and ready to head back to the hospital. "Considering I didn't get home until 3 a.m., I had to be running on adrenalin, and I still didn't know if I'd be allowed into the hospital," Bruce said. "COVID rules or not, I was going to get in and see Barb."

"Our cat, Oscar, was sadly being ignored," Bruce said. "He did his best to give me the attention he generally reserves only for Barb. And, poor little guy, I have no recollection of how or if he got fed or his water dish refilled over those first few days."

Wearily driving back to the hospital in Uptown Charlotte, Bruce says he kept rethinking each step of the night before. "I was playing the "what if" game," he tells me, "What if we had made it home and into bed before your stroke hit. Considering all the wine we had consumed, I can imagine sleeping right through it and only waking to find you gone," Bruce said, tearing up.

But, by the grace of God, I was not gone. And Bruce was able to negotiate his way into my ICU room. That's my Bruce!

"You looked like hell," he tells me bluntly now. He even snapped this lovely picture to show family and friends that I was alive.

Thankful to see me still breathing, he honestly feared for what was left of me seeing my condition.

"The nurses helped me track down Barb's doctor who provided a quick recap on her condition," Bruce said, "With terms I did not completely understand at that point."

But he did learn that the anterior stroke I suffered impacted my brain's right side. In addition, it had affected my eyesight, and there was no movement in my left arm or leg. The extent of these problems and more would be assessed in the coming hours and days.

What happened after the doctor left is the memory I

prefer to remember.

I guess deciding there was little he could do at that point, Bruce began gently stroking my hair, saying, "Everything will be okay, Barb." And then he sang my favorite song to me.

You are my Sunshine,
my only Sunshine.
You make me happy when skies are gray.
You'll never know, dear, how much I love you,
please don't take my Sunshine away.

"As her breathing softened, I heard a rustle of someone behind me. A tear was rolling down the cheek of the nurse standing there," Bruce said.

During the long hours of watching and waiting in the ICU that first day, Bruce took calls from our family and answered their questions about my condition as best he could. When he finally figured out how to log into my online medical records, he was able to read the ER and surgeon notes from my first night.

The report was still full of the medical jargon he did not wholly understand. The notes made it obvious the effort to remove the clots in two areas, my cerebral and carotid arteries, was very complicated. It took numerous attempts to get the catheter into the accurate pathway to get the blood flowing again. In addition, the stroke had done severe damage to the right side of my brain, leaving 30% of my brain cells dead...forever.

I was numb from all the drugs they were pumping into my system, but Bruce says reading about my surgery made him feel numb, too. What would this mean to my future? What would this mean to our future?

> For those of you who do not know us,
> allow me to take a step back into our past...
> way back, to introduce ourselves.

I'm Barbara, Barb to my friends, and the youngest of two children in my family, with my brother Tom, seven years older. We had very loving parents, Floyd and Ruth Byron, and I had lots of friends. Growing up in Saginaw, Michigan, on the river's west side was idyllic.

"Barb was a cute short blonde, and she was spoiled rotten," Bruce always says. And I'll admit, I was popular, but I gained an endless sense of optimism and empathy for others based on the example my parents provided.

In ways, the Kwaiser family was the mirror image of the Byron's. They lived on Saginaw's west side, Bruce was the youngest, and his "perfect" sister Janet was seven years his senior. Bruce attended a different elementary and middle school, but we both attended Arthur Hill high school, just a block away from the Kwaiser home.

Bruce had this twinkle in his eye from a young age, and he lived life to the fullest. Janet says Bruce was even caught looking up the girls' skirts at kindergarten rest time and had to take his rest time in front of the principal's desk after that.

By his early teens, he played nearly every sport, rode motor scooters, and caught the eye of all the girls in school.

I'll never forget when my dad and I drove by Bruce catching a ride on his buddy's motor scooter. I guess I was checking out his muscular rear end, still in his basketball uniform, as my dad cleared his throat loudly. I'm sure I turned 18 shades of red.

By the time I entered tenth grade, and Bruce was in eleventh and a junior, we were dating. Our classes were quite large, and everyone wanted to know how we met or who introduced us. "We were never introduced," I liked to say because I just always knew who he was.

I was the one who got the ball rolling when we had a "turn-about party" where the girls invited boys to a dance. Thus began our courtship that has now lasted over 60 years.

Enough about the past for now. Let's get back
to me lying helpless in the hospital.

I spent three days in the ICU and then moved to another floor and to three separate rooms over the next seven days. The increase in COVID cases was causing havoc with hospital administration of rooms and staffing.

I grew weary of the repeated requests to "Tell me your name." "What's your date of birth?" "Where are you?" "What is today's date?"

While I was grateful to be alive, I had lost all mobility on my left side. At this point, I had little ability to move overall, and speaking was challenging. In addition, the stroke had impacted peripheral vision in my eyes, and being a voracious reader, this really upset me.

I overheard the nurses telling Bruce I would have to relearn virtually everything and require hands-on care forever. Bruce looked scared. It was then the Annie and Pollyanna spirit that had gotten me through life this far kicked in. 'Tomorrow is only a day away,' I would tell myself.

Those ten days in the hospital were my first tiny steps in relearning virtually everything. Starting with how to chew and swallow, an occupational therapist or aide was with me for every meal. That is if you consider colored mush a meal.

I had to relearn how to feed myself and eat the mush without choking. Fortunately, I'm right-handed. Can you imagine how much more difficult this would be for a left-hander? I still must hunt for the food on the left side of my plate.

I became capable of finding a few words to express how I was feeling, which felt like a big deal. The OT could understand which colors of mush I hated and which I could tolerate. So, she would play this game with me, where she would place the mush I liked best off to my left side. Since I had no peripheral vision, this challenged me to turn my eyes and body to find it. Those sneaky therapists would do the same thing with the television remote control, so I would figure out which show they liked and switch it on to see them smile.

Having a stroke affects many more people
than just the patient.

The early days were apparently a blur for Bruce, traveling back and forth to the hospital and raising hell if he thought something was lacking in the attention I was getting. But, of course, the worst COVID cases were being directed to this trauma center, so I'm not surprised the nurses were feeling overwhelmed. And, because of pandemic restrictions, no visitors were allowed besides Bruce, so there was no relief for him.

One thing Bruce did manage to do was stop by to thank the EMT crew who delivered me safely to CMC that frightening evening. He apologized for the mess they had to clean up after me. They laughed and said there had been worse clean-ups.

When Bruce was not visiting me, he was busy researching everything he could about "cerebrovascular accident," the medical name for a stroke. And all the other medical terms related to the anterior stroke that had severely impacted the right hemisphere of my brain.

The report conveyed: The ventricular arrhythmia or atrial fibrillation that caused the development of a clot in my heart was sent through the artery to my brain. And, it most certainly had its genesis with plaque buildup.

His sister Janet, a nurse, and Ph. D. was helping him scour the internet and books to understand symptoms, tests, treatments, and rehabilitation therapy options. They wanted to learn what progress they should expect to see from me and what was required from my caregivers and care facilities.

Bruce knew how I would want things handled if it went downhill because we had those conversations before. But he also knew hospitals must have it in writing so he located our medical directive papers all the while praying there would be no need to refer to them.

I never worried I was dying. I told my minister and friend Mark Pitts, "I feel like I am in a good place with God." While the words probably came out still slurred, he seemed to understand. I felt then and still feel that I'm just a little piece of His big plan. Along with my caregivers, we are all doing our part in that plan.

You might be wondering how you go from dating in 10th grade to still being together after 60 years.

Bruce and I were not yet out of high school when we

married. It was a family-only ceremony held at the Lutheran church where the Kwaiser family belonged. I was only 17 and Bruce 18, but I was pregnant, and we were committed to spending our lives together. We were also committed to graduating from college. We didn't know enough to be afraid of the future.

Our son, Steve, was born in 1962, the year we enrolled in Michigan State University, where I majored in teaching and Bruce in business marketing. We lived in married student housing on campus, where most of the other residents were grad students. In retrospect this was probably the easiest period of our married life even with Steve waking up at 4 a.m.

Following our son, Steve, came daughter Kris, born in 1969. The same lucky seven-year age difference both Bruce and I had with our siblings.

Flash forwards some 50 years; we love being "Nonie" and "Grampy" to our granddaughter, McKenzie, Kris and Kip's daughter, and Stephanie and Dylan, Steve's kids. We've even added three precious great-grandchildren, Brooke, Avery, and Jason. But, of course, sometimes they call Bruce "Grumpy," and I say if the shoe fits...

The moniker "Nonie" came to me during a trip to Arizona, where a Navajo Indian guide shared the deep history of his people. I asked how he acquired all this knowledge and expected to hear that his father and male elders gave him this schooling. But he proudly explained that his ancestral knowledge and traditions were from his Nonie, or grandmother, who was the family member committed to keeping their family story passed through the generations. So, I decided I wanted to be the "Nonie" for my growing family. With tons of genealogy research, I've traced my family's roots back to the 1500s in England and Bruce's family back to the 1800s, immigrating from Russia.

Following my dad's advice to "make a friend in every place you move," our circle of friends now covers the U.S. Naturally, we focus more on local friends since Bruce has retired. I'm incredibly close with my girlfriends in my two book clubs, Bruce has his golf buddies, and then there are our Lake Norman neighborhood friends.

We are immensely proud of the life we have built together. We stuck together as teenagers becoming parents, achieved our college degrees while figuring out how to raise a child, and survived through nine corporate moves.

"After 60 years of marriage, we have never felt more in love," Bruce says, and I feel the same.

I realize that having loving parents and faith in God has given me the foundation that guides me now. And having amassed a set of close friends that I like to think of as an opera-length set of pearls gives me support and strength through all of life's good times and bad.

Bruce adds, "Life is a set of choices, some harder than others. But I am eternally grateful that I chose Barb and Barb chose me."

TIP FROM BARB

5

To help you interpret medical jargon, just repeat what you are told…but put it into your own words, to ensure you got it right.

Follow the professional's recommendations and don't be afraid to ask questions.

TIP FROM BARB

6

What is your name?
Your date of birth?
Today's date?
Where are you?

You will get sick of these questions,
but try to know the answers.

Yet, to my mind, doesn't "Where are you" depend?
Surprise your nurse with this question: "Do you mean
yesterday, last week, tomorrow or right at this moment?"

BARB'S QUIPS

"I'm somewhere between
Annie and Pollyanna.

Annie believes tomorrow is another day.
Pollyanna is happy with whatever is given her, including
crutches ... even if she doesn't have to use them."

BARB'S QUIPS

*Advice I learned early
from my parents:*

"If today's not good,
there is always tomorrow."

"Don't make judgements until you've walked
a mile in the other person's shoes."

"Laugh and the world
laughs with you.
Cry, and you cry alone."

DAY 11 TO DAY 31: BARB

ACUTE REHABILITATION

After a 10-day hospital stay you might think I was thrilled to get out. But my graduation...can you believe they call it that...was to an acute rehabilitation center which is much like a hospital. The specialized center was in Mount Holly, North Carolina where I would spend the next 21 days. Like hospital care, this was fully supported by Medicare and my insurance.

I was happy to continue working on my recovery, but I was not happy about the COVID restrictions they again placed on Bruce. He was allowed only two hours of visitation each day, from 3:00-5:00 p.m. This meant he would be fighting our city commute traffic to get home every night, something we retired folks avoid at all costs. And I was also concerned for Bruce since there was no one to come home to and no meal on the table when he got there.

Acute rehabilitation is much like it sounds, intensive amounts of therapy and treatment. I had received speech, occupational and physical therapy at the hospital, but it became more intensive in acute rehab.

Here I was receiving at least three hours of rigorous speech, occupational and physical therapy each day. For example, therapy targeted my left side awareness and speech. I struggled to see words on the left side of a written page and found word puzzles challenging, so we worked a lot on that.

The work I put in was showing improvement every day. But there were times when I thought, can't you just show me how to use the remote?

I found that the right brain impact of my stroke meant my brain couldn't always direct my body to do what my mind was thinking. For example, I would tell my morning nurse I spent the night out dancing. But she would just look at me like I was nuts because I couldn't smile or wink at the same time to let her know I was just joking.

Plus, I could only imagine the look I wanted to give the aides who brought tasteless scrambled eggs for breakfast day after day after day. It was enough having scrambled brains; I did not need the reminder.

That's why it made my day when my daughter Kris would sneak in with a McDonald's or a Chick-fil-A lunch. This was a waste of money because swallowing was still a huge effort and there was no way I could eat real food. But I appreciated the milkshakes, the other aromas, and her effort.

> As a good student and education major, I was frustrated by my pace of PT and OT learning. Yet, I tried to keep my sunny side up.

When you grow up the daughter of Floyd Byron, kids write in your *slam book*, "Of course you get all A's. You're the principal's daughter!" But I did not let the slam bother me because I was proud of my straight A's, even if they came easy to me. While I didn't always love being the principal's daughter, I certainly loved my dad.

Beginning at age five, Dad and I made weekly visits to the library. I cherished the time alone with him. Dad would settle in to read newspapers and periodicals, while I would go challenge the librarian.

The librarian referred to me as an "A-to-Z reader" because I devoured all the book series, like *Sue Barton* and *Cherry Ames*. She would groan when she saw me coming, asking her to help me find something I had not already read on the shelf. Yet, I often needed Dad's assistance carrying my stack of library books home each week.

Other times with Dad was work. He recruited me to help shovel snow off our sidewalk and the neighbor's walk before dawn on wintry school days. Then Dad would drive us to the schoolhouse singing, *Oh What a Beautiful Morning*, despite the grey skies. His mission as the school principal was to start everyone's day off on a good note by helping the neighbors and making a pot of coffee for the janitors and teachers.

His example of working hard and doing for others was not lost on me and is certainly paying off now.

> Bruce continued to have his own
> frustrations to bear.

During my acute rehab days, Bruce realized "this" wasn't going away. I was making progress, but it was slow. Having reached the limitations of our insurance coverage, I was again going to graduate to the next level: skilled care. One of these days I'm expecting a cap and gown.

Bruce was the one who shouldered the burden of figuring out where to go next. Negotiating with the insurance companies, researching treatment options and the facilities offering them, was like his new career.

> I knew I could trust Bruce as my medical
> system navigator while I focused on my rehab.
> We were always a good team.

Right out of college, Bruce landed a job with Dow Chemical in sales. We were immediately sent to Boston, where Bruce trained in their packaging division. As his career developed, we were moved about every three to four years during his 34 years with Dow, finally retiring in 1999 in Mooresville, North Carolina on Lake Norman. It was a good run for both of us.

"The Stepford Wives" was the nickname my girlfriend Charlotte gave the wives after we were subjected to a talk from Dow's human resource executive. He had gathered a group of Dow Chemical managers' wives to instruct us on our critical role in our husband's careers. "You can turn down a move anytime you wish," he told us, "But after you do, we will begin to recognize the fence you have built around yourselves," inferring it would hamper our spouse's career advancement if we did. As for the Kwaiser's, we never built that fence and moved nine times for "The Dow." While the moves were challenging, it allowed us to make lasting friendships in every city.

When we lived in Midland, Michigan, Dow headquarters, we did a lot of home entertaining as none of us had the money to frequent restaurants. There was a party trick we followed to put $5 in a hat if you mentioned Dow. The guys often got caught and were forced to pay up, but I felt it kept them from "talking shop" after hours.

My job was to set up a comfortable household in each new location and guide our kids into a new school and friendships. But this also meant giving up on my full-time teaching career, replacing it with substitute teaching when my schedule allowed. I joined Welcome Wagon, the local church, and baked cookies and bread for Kris to deliver to new neighbors...a way for her to start making friends.

Managing the home front while Bruce traveled for the week, I perfected the fine art of presenting the kids with choices rather than giving them orders. "Would you like me to save some French fries for you, Steve? Or have the oil nice and hot to make a fresh batch when you finish that last bit of lawn mowing?" I would ask our young son who was dragging his feet on his lawn chores. Fresh hot fries got the job done every time.

I also mastered the balance of work with pleasure, believing 20 minutes of ironing earned me a couple of chapters in my book of the moment. My love of reading motivated me to be active in two book clubs, generating a tremendous support system of friends I would need in the years to come.

TIP FROM BARB

7

Join or form a book club.

If you are an avid reader like me, discussing the books you read with good friends is one of life's greatest pleasures.

And thank goodness there are audio books for when a stroke messes with your eyesight and reading books is no longer an option. (Free with a library card and listening app.)

BARB'S QUIPS

"Ouch!"

"You do that again and you might just wind up on page 42 of my book.

DAY 32 TO DAY 77: BRUCE

SKILLED CARE

I cringe when recalling Barb's move into a Cornelius, North Carolina skilled care facility. Barb still required 75 percent or more of all care done for her. So, despite graduating from acute care, she was very dependent on caregiving professionals. Still, professional is the last word I would describe the culture at this facility. I'll resist even naming the place.

Barb was restricted from all visitors for the initial 14 days, including me, per state COVID requirements in place at the time. Then, when a patient or staff member was diagnosed with COVID, another 14-day shutdown to visitors went into force. This could have left me totally in the dark on her quality of care, but she was on the ground floor where I could peer in through the window. Barb could also speed dial me on her cell phone, although our conversations were limited by her still impaired speech.

However, my worst nightmare came true based on what

I saw through that window. So, let me start at the beginning.

We transferred Barb via private pay ambulance to this skilled care facility with a suitcase and a couple boxes. I was forced to leave her at the door, per the COVID rules, and let the staff get her settled.

After moving into her room, the first thing Barb asked was to use the bathroom. A staff member got Barb onto the toilet and left the room. Within seconds of her leaving, Barb fell to the floor, lying crumpled against the wall until the aide returned. Clearly, her discharge information from the prior facility had not been read, and obviously, this staff member had used poor judgment. Barb required assistance sitting upright at this point and everything else associated with toileting. It was evident to anyone. If you were paying attention.

Their solution was to write new orders requiring two staff members to assist Barb in toileting and bathing. Still, since two staff members were virtually never available when needed, she spent way too much time in a diaper...a wet diaper. Barb was not given a full shower until six days after arrival. It was not long before she developed sores and a bladder infection.

Three days after her arrival, I came to Barb's window and saw her slumped down in her wheelchair, nearly falling off and screaming, "HEEELP!"

I immediately called the nurses station, but no one answered. I then called the front desk and insisted they get someone to attend to her immediately. Another five to eight minutes went by, and still nothing.

I called the front desk again and said if someone didn't get in there to help my wife, I would have to call 911. Their reaction was to chastise me for my bad behavior. Things happened relatively fast then, but it still took about five minutes before Barb was rescued from her wheelchair and her diaper changed.

To spare you more sad details, let me jump to my solution. I hired a private licensed caregiver, who would have to be admitted into the facility and Barb's room. This would give me eyes on Barb and a report back on any concerns.

The reports were not good. The worst news was that Barb was getting very depressed, and our hired aide reported Barb felt like she was in prison. She would press her call button for help at night and be told, "Just go to sleep."

So, after only 45 days in the disappointing location, with 30 of those days in COVID isolation, I decided to move Barb again.

I realized the skilled care system is designed for the patient, but it is far from a perfect system. Care facilities vary significantly in their actual "caring". It was all-consuming making sure the poorly supervised and overwhelmed staff was paying attention to Barb's needs.

I felt I had no option but to oversee everything from choosing the clothes Barb would wear to scheduling visits around pandemic regulations to ensuring Barb was bathed and fed appropriately. Friends kept reminding me I had to also take care of myself. Yeah, right, I thought, in my spare time.

> This is Barb's story, but you might want to know more about my story for all those spouses out there trying to keep it together.

You may recall, back on Day 1, you learned I had prostate cancer. So, I was already accustomed to spending my days researching medical care options and weighing the insurance and financial implications. We were all set to leave January 3 for Atlanta and the lengthy proton radiation treatment scheduled. That plan now came to a screeching halt.

I ended up canceling the proton radiation procedure I had chosen and went back to the initial plan which was the intensive modulated external beam therapy and hormone treatments available in Charlotte. During this chaotic time with Barb's recovery, I still needed to get things going on my prostate cancer treatment, as my Gleason scores deemed it a very aggressive cancer.

So, in my "spare time," I hustled into Charlotte for

treatment and back to Barb's window or home to make calls and oversee her care.

My treatment resulted in the painful side effect of lymphedema. Not something I shared with Barb, who was enduring her own pain.

The effects of stress caused both PMR (polymyalgia rheumatica) and shingles. The PMR was very scary and took a while to diagnose, and yes, I did have the shingles vaccine. This stuff was occurring on top of the knee surgery I had the prior September and shoulder problem that got worse in November. As an avid golfer, to have my clubs collecting dust and my last posted golf game October 12, 2020, meant life was dreary.

My doctors and friends urged me to concentrate on my care, but I couldn't rest until Barb received proper care.

> Craving the memory of happier times, I would try to remember the early days when we were both healthy and the future was our oyster.

Still underage for drinking, my brother-in-law Wayne would visit us on campus at Michigan State and bring a case of beer. What a treat, even if it was cheap Land of Lakes. Wayne and my sister Janet taught us to play bridge during these visits, which turned out to be an affordable and fun way to entertain other couples. We both loved the game, especially Barb.

Juggling classes and parenting, we occasionally squeezed in time to hang out with former high school classmates who were enjoying the single fraternity and sorority life. It was easy to feel jealous, but we turned our attention to potential new friends who could enhance our expanding horizons.

The paper-thin walls of married student housing allowed a way to "know" neighbors and help each other look after each other's infants. Barb met a woman from India. Excited to learn about her culture and spend time together, Barb was ultimately appalled to observe the woman refusing to associate with a fellow India exchange student because she came from a lower caste. Barb rejected her friendship and continued her search for people who shared our values, were well-traveled, educated, open-minded, and encouraged one another; what Barb later referred to as people like us, or "PLU."

Fast forward to even happier times.

By 2000, we were enjoying retirement. I would hop on our boat for the five-minute drive to our country club. After tethering the boat, a caddy would be there to welcome me with a ride to the pro shop and my tee time with my best golf buddies. I pinched myself every time, thinking, "Is this really happening to a guy from Saginaw?"

DAY 32 TO DAY 77: BARB

SKILLED CARE

My first 45 days in skilled care were a considerable low point. The pandemic restrictions meant I endured long and lonely days in my room. The staffing problems were exacerbated by the strict rules and limited my care drastically compared to acute care.

I was not alone in my misery. I could hear other patients up and down the hallway calling for help throughout the day and night.

Staring out my window was bleak during these wintry days, so you can imagine my thrill when visitors surprised me with window visits. Granddaughter Stephanie and grandson Dylan and their families, as well as some neighbors with their kids came and taped artwork to my window.

Debbie brought my favorite chocolate chip cookies and had to leave them at the front desk for me. I shared them with my OT and PT therapists over a cup of coffee to entice them to stay longer. Their three times a week therapy was okay, but the company was better.

Bruce would also arrive at my window when he wasn't allowed in. Still, the visits from all were awkward. They would peer at me in my wheelchair and attempt small talk on cell phones. I missed the hugs and casual conversation.

The staff used to comment on all the texts and emails I got and wondered why I left my busy phone lying on my lap. "You would, too, if you set your phone on vibrate." I'd tell them just to see them blush.

Making friends has long been a priority for me.
And loads of fun.

Some of Bruce's bravado rubbed off on me when we joined the high school fraternity and sorority groups forbidden to meet on high school property. Something my dad, the principal, and my conservative Mom reluctantly agreed to.

I was named Sergeant of Arms for my sorority since I was a good rule enforcer...even though my sorority sisters and I occasionally broke the school rules.

Our groups liked to party on Lake Huron with bonfires on the beach. Our favorite spot was next to a cemetery, where the guys strategically dug a pit for the beer. They figured it would be quick to cover up if the authorities arrived and hoped they wouldn't look in a cemetery for our contraband.

I will not forget the night the cops did arrive, and partiers scattered everywhere, behind headstones and down the beach in all directions. Fortunately, I was a champion in the 75-yard dash, so I sprinted along with my friend Margaret to Mom's borrowed car to escape. It was a white 1959 Chevy convertible with cherry red interior. The same head turning car I let Bruce drive on our first date.

Margaret and I evaded the police and made it back to my family's cabin, where my parents played bridge and were none the wiser of our escapades. I am so grateful my memories and recollections of these raucous times are still with me.

*When life throws you hard-boiled eggs,
make a great egg salad sandwich.*

A stroke was not my first major health issue. In January of 2000, I got the news no woman wants to hear: "You have breast cancer." It would be a rough five-year treatment journey, but I had Bruce and family at my side.

After grueling cancer treatments, Bruce decided a Caribbean cruise was my needed distraction. I was not sure I was up for it, but cherished Bruce's support. So, I packed my brunette, blonde, and highlighted wigs, and off we went.

Onboard the ship that night, we were seated for dinner

with a physically disabled 23-yr old and her father. I had acquired a sixth sense of what people need by this point in my life and, sensing the strain in their relationship, I deduced they were trying to reconnect. Learning a horse accident had caused her disability, I thought of our daughter Kris' love of horses and vowed to help the young girl.

Also joining us for dinner was a young couple from Greenville, SC. I asked the couple if they were celebrating anything on the cruise. Looking into the dark eyes of the young wife, I realized that was not the case. I learned of her recent miscarriage with a few quietly exchanged words and sensed possible postpartum depression.

Reflecting on what I was learning about the group, I thought what a dysfunctional group we find ourselves with, and with my cancer, I'm also part of the dysfunction. Yet I felt God put me here for a reason. So, I discreetly cut the meat for the young girl and prompted Bruce to share a funny story about us to lighten the mood and bring joy to the group.

> Making new friends is a lifelong pleasure,
> especially girlfriends.

My friend Charlotte was going through a divorce and turning 50, so she needed cheering up. Since my cruise had cheered me up, a group of us put together a surprise birthday cruise for Charlotte.

It was on the ship Ecstasy, aptly named as we wanted to celebrate the beauty that Charlotte was. Coincidentally, several of us were reading *Divine Secrets of the Ya-Ya Sisterhood* and were inspired by their Southern charm. When the ship docked in Nassau, we bought puka beads, dubbed them our pearls, and practiced our Southern 'touch and wave' technique as we departed port that evening. We became famous onboard for our charm and decided to carry over our bond with the formation of The Pearlie Girls book club when we returned. The group has been together 22 years now and has served as a very special group that has supported many life challenges.

BARB'S QUIPS

"When you don't like the situation you are in...
Just piss on it!"

But it helps if you are wearing Depends.

BARB'S QUTPS

My response to the nurse inserting a catheter for a UTI exam; when she asked if I was allergic to seafood:

"What are you planning to do?

Put a shrimp in my hoo-hah?!"

BARB'S QUIPS

"Biofreeze won't stop perspiration."

I found this out when a distracted caregiver applied it instead of my deodorant one day.

DAY 78 TO DAY 266: BRUCE

SKILLED CARE #2

Barb's stay in the first skilled care facility was yielding no improvement at a time that was considered critical days for relearning. Plus, the energy I was pouring into resolving all the issues took its toll on me. It was time for a change.

There was a time when Barb and I imagined downsizing to The Pines at Davidson which is a continuing care community. It had beautiful independent homes and apartments for seniors and a great reputation. While once a plan we dreamed of, our nightmare now demanded a new look at our long-term strategy.

I headed over to examine The Pines skilled care, something we hadn't studied carefully before. This option came at a significantly higher cost and was not Medicare approved, but I could no longer tolerate inferior alternatives. The Pines fortunately had an open room so we packed Barb into an ambulance for the third time and moved.

The costlier decision was more than rewarded with the

quality of care. A shining example was The Pines social worker, Connie. She advised me to request a compassionate care designation, allowing me to bypass COVID rules and gain immediate and daily access to Barb.

Connie also directed me to Alison at Gaitway Group for highly rated occupational and physical therapy. Based on Barb's needs, Alison assigned Kelly for physical therapy and Cindy for occupational therapy who each provided one hour per day, five days a week, for six months. This was also private pay, so at a significantly greater cost, but Connie and Alison's advice vastly improved the care and therapy Barb received and her outlook.

DAY 78 TO DAY 266: BARB

SKILLED CARE #2

Kelly and Cindy, my therapists from Gaitway, became my cheerleaders and later, best friends. They helped me recover so many skills I had taken for granted before my stroke. We began at a point where I still couldn't sit up in bed by myself, and they helped me progress in my recovery to walking 175 feet with the use of an upright hemi-walker.

They encouraged my eating and swallowing activities and supervised many hours of intensive and productive therapy. While it was hard work, we often laughed until we were all in tears.

Alison, the owner of the therapy group, regularly checked in on both my satisfaction and Bruce's. She wrote letters to help Bruce make medical claims. Bruce and I came to refer to Connie, Alison, Kelly, and Cindy as the new Pearls in our lives.

"Barb's determination to work hard on her therapy and always bring her jolly self is my inspiration," said Bruce, "And this team helped Barb out of her depression and charge forward."

One of the most important things they taught me was to put safety first. After previous falls, this was just what I needed. I learned to try new things following risk/reward considerations. There was no point in learning to stand up, only to fall and regress in my recovery.

Even the best skilled care is still like an institution.

Finally, COVID restrictions were easing, and my level of independence was improving. For example, I could join other skilled care residents in the dining room for meals, yet conversation with some residents was another matter.

One woman would ask repeatedly, and of no one in particular, "Have you seen my husband?" My efforts to console the woman I learned was a widow were not working, so I'd eventually suggest asking a nurse for help. A gentleman thought he was in a hotel and kept asking, "When is check-out time?" Again, I tried to help but suggested asking a nurse.

Witnessing this gave me great respect for the caregivers' patience, talent, and gentle spirit in working with the residents. However, it also dismayed me wondering how long this would be my home.

Time to show off my new skills and reintroduce

ourselves to the grands and greats.

One celebratory decision Bruce and I made was arranging a family trip to Holden Beach, North Carolina. It had been four months since my stroke, and Bruce decided I needed a change of scenery. COVID restrictions meant we had little contact with our family since the stroke.

The family, now numbering 13, all made the trip. That alone was an accomplishment.

Our week together was filled with sun, fun, and lots of laughs. My heart sings knowing that our grands and great-grands enjoy their lives and have genuinely fantastic parents. And I sit taller with pride after each interaction. I just wish it were more frequent.

Back to my tiny skilled care room
and my new normal.

Finally, a few more visits were allowed if everyone wore a mask and kept their distance. Small groups from both my book clubs and neighbors paid short visits. Friends who also lived at The Pines stopped by more often, which brightened my day and were a welcome diversion from the ominous hum of a skilled care setting. But again, I agonized, how long would I have to be here? Do I even have an option?

There are days when Bruce asked, "What's the status of your brain today," and I'd say it's a gray fuzzy day. Yet, I liked to imagine my good brain cells sweeping away the bad cells on those days. Like an Olympic curler, I swept away the gray to help my memory and thoughts hit the target.

Bright lights hurt my eyes, although the sun doesn't, oddly. I still can't see words, food, or anything much on my left side. This keeps me from being a candidate for a motorized wheelchair since I would become a traffic risk, but my goal is to leave wheelchairs behind.

My mom died of a stroke the same age as mine. So, all these inconveniences I suffer are just aggravations, I remind myself. Every day I wake, I thank the Lord her fate is not mine.

TIP FROM BARB

8

Make use of Social Workers in the medical system.

Most hospitals, acute care, and skilled care facilities have social workers who are your advocates. They help interpret the jargon you are hearing.

Social workers help
navigate care options and resources, both
within the facility and outside.

DAY 267 TO TODAY: BRUCE

INDEPENDENT LIVING WITH HELP

After seven and a half months, the financial impact of Barb's care, especially private pay skilled care, and private pay therapy, plus my own medical care, was taking its toll. Financing the amenities of our old life, which was now on hold, was also something we could not sustain.

Mainly we did not want to keep living apart. I was determined to find a way we could live together. Based on my investigation, Barb's care needs meant finding a continuing care facility that would accept Barb in independent living quarters.

The most significant change we would need to accept is I would become Barb's primary caregiver. While Barb's life had already changed forever, I realized my life would also radically change.

Taking on this huge commitment, I thought it might be easier if we were closer to our daughter Kris in Greenville, South Carolina. Barb had already been away from our Mooresville home for seven and a half months, but this move meant we would both have to give up the neighborhood we had lived in for 30 years. We built a good life here with dozens of friends and neighbors, the yard I loved to tend, my incredible golf buddies, our church, doctors we trusted, and more. It was a frightening prospect.

Our move decision was made better with consultation from Barb's trusted therapy team leader, Alison, who traveled to Greenville for a first-hand inspection. We were drawn to the patio homes at Rolling Greens Village, but Alison pointed out that with Barb still in a wheelchair, it was not practical for her to ride in a golf cart to the main building for dining and activities.

We finally opted for a two-bedroom apartment in the main building. It had a full kitchen, an office area to call my own, a bedroom we could finally share again, and flexibility for the independence we hoped Barb would continue to acquire.

So, I bit the bullet and put our beautiful retirement home on the market. With help from our friends to clean, box, and move our belongings, we now live two and a half hours south in Greenville.

Since our new apartment was one-quarter the size of our family home, many things were donated to local charities or stored. Unfortunately, the kids and grands wanted very few of the cherished items we tried to gift them. In our haste to pack up the house, with the assistance of my well-meaning buddies, belongings got tossed into moving boxes without labels.

By day 267 in Barb's recovery, we were welcomed into our new apartment, and the scavenger hunt for missing items began.

DAY 267 TO TODAY: BARB

THIS IS OUR LIFE NOW

There is an expansive view out our third-floor balcony. But the view I like better is company walking through the front door.

I can count on an aide coming through our front door in the morning. They are here seven days a week to help me use the bathroom, get showered, dressed, and walk the hallways.

After one full year of PT and OT, doctors assessed that I hit a plateau. But I don't listen to them, and neither should you. Experienced rehab therapists tell me you can achieve improvements for years and years. So, I am committed to continuing therapy on my own with the help and encouragement of those around me. Bruce is my motivator and hires and supervises the therapists and aides who help.

When a new aide arrives to start my day, I try to remember the words of my cheerleading therapists, Kelly, and Cindy. Let's put it this way, some aides are better than others. But they do help strap me onto a modified walker and take a 15-minute walk up and down the hallway. Longer on good days.

Bruce is my one trusted constant. Kris helps when her schedule allows, but she is a busy woman.

I'm immensely proud of Bruce for taking on all the tasks of the household, plus serving as my caretaker when the aides leave at noon. After 60 years of marriage, he finally learned how to do laundry, prepare most of the food we have in our room, do all our shopping, even how to buy a bra. He also makes a great omelet.

We are working hard on making new friends in our new home and staying in touch with our old friends. As time goes on, contact diminishes, which we know is normal. You know how it goes. We are no longer at our old social get-togethers and new memories are formed without us. But I keep reassuring Bruce that we are in their thoughts.

Don't feel bad for me, I have exciting news.

My goal is to walk to our community dining room without the aid of my walker. The exciting news is I have already graduated from my walker to a quad-cane. Soon I expect to use the quad-cane without the assistance of someone hanging onto my waist belt. A graduation worthy of a cap and gown.

Keeping joy in our hearts and movement forward.

We do like to think back on our Saginaw, Michigan beginning and the start of our loving relationship. I value the incessant optimism my parents taught me.

There are so many crazy and fun memories Bruce and I share. Like the Harley he bought in retirement, the long road trips, and fantastic folks we met along the way. Bruce wore a t-shirt saying, "If you can read this, the bitch fell off," and my shirt said, "I'm the bitch who fell off."

While my stroke sometimes makes me feel like I did fall off that bike, I did survive. And I am moving forward. We try to make more tame and better choices these days. Although I do have some fun pet names for select caregivers, I could share with you privately.

We strive to eat healthier smaller meals and get more exercise, yet old habits are hard to break. We are also returning to card games, using the card holding gizmo my old bridge partner Fern got for me. Bruce really misses golf but plans to try playing again soon. And we love socializing as a couple again. We lean on our faith and our friends in equal proportion.

The friends we spent a lifetime cultivating across the country have stuck with us. "Our friends are our rock," Bruce adds. And, we have both become much closer to our Lord.

> You need help from more than the medical system and your loving partner when you have a stroke.

We are sure we could not, in any way, have gotten through the early days and months that followed my stroke without our fantastic friends. I call them my "Pearls," and Bruce does the same when referring to our most cherished people.

I am eternally grateful to Cathy, who recognized the stroke immediately and had her husband, Jim, call 911 and then drive Bruce to the ER. His friend Bob, who was also at his side during my ER stay, continues to check in with Bruce, every single day...yes, every single day.

As news of our situation quickly spread, Bruce started an email update and expanded it to include friends from coast to coast. Pastor Mark put us on our church prayer list, and Bruce and I swear we could feel its power.

Cards, letters, and emails of concern poured in.

They came from book club friends, business friends, neighbors, country club friends, church friends, and even from our friends' children. It is astounding how they have kept tabs on us as I've made all these moves.

Bruce would probably not have eaten, or undoubtedly not well, were it not for the friends who invited him to dinner or filled our refrigerator with prepared meals.

"On some nights, I felt too exhausted to go out, but friends still encouraged me to dine with them, and the warm company and sense of normalcy turned out to be exactly what I needed," Bruce confirmed.

"I realize, even saying this now, that I probably should have asked them to do more...as the generic offer to, 'Let me know how I can help,' could have been turned into relief I could have used," Bruce added.

I've lost a lot, like the purse I lost on stroke night and even my wedding rings. Bruce assures me that they will turn up in a moving box and it will be just like Christmas. But for now, belongings are floating around in the universe, waiting to be found. Just like me and our old life.

TIP FROM BARB

9

Strokes can be avoided.

The phrase, "Do what I say, not what I do," could apply here. I've learned more about lifestyle choices you can make to avoid having a stroke. But finding the motivation to change is easier said than done.

Does this always work? Ask Jill Bolte Taylor, the brain scientist who suffered her own stroke at the age of 37. You cannot always avoid a stroke, but read her book, *My Stroke of Insight*, and learn more about what you can do.

Get motivated now, or you might be writing a book like this, as well.

TIP FROM BARB

10

Every woman needs a place to
call home...

Our home went from a 5,000 sq. ft. home in Mooresville to a 1,000 sq. ft. apartment in Greenville, but Bruce and I are still together, and home is where my heart is.

...but you also need a place to
run away to.

The family cabin at Tawas, Michigan, was where I took the kids for getaways over the years. Today, the first-floor handicap-access bedroom that daughter Kris added to her new house serves as my escape.

TIP FROM BARB

11

Get ready for a scavenger hunt.

Emergency room visits and moves from one care center to another can leave your belongings in perpetual motion or lost forever.

When you can't go searching by yourself, get good at directing. Gone are the days when you jump in the car alone and go anywhere.

TIP FROM BARB

12

Learn to instruct your husband on
how to shop for a bra.

There will likely be many returns until he finds the right size and style as he discovers hooks, snaps, and zippers and more options than he knew existed.

TIP FROM BARB

13

Get yourself a Mr. Uber.

If you are not fortunate enough to have married him 60 years ago, find someone you can call upon for help.

And to help him become a pro at sequencing. For example, when he's wheeling you to the bathroom, roll by the Kleenex box and grab a few for later, and the remote control.

Then give him a good review because he's a pretty good guy.

TIP FROM BARB

14

A great way to meet new people in your new residence: Volunteer

In Rolling Green, resident volunteers provide meal delivery to other residents' apartments. This gives folks a way to get to know each other.

We established a wine and appetizer get-together for those without family on Christmas Eve and continue it weekly, along with a Euchre group we started.

I plan to start a store called "Spare Wheels" to find new homes for the equipment I no longer need.

BARB'S QUIPS

"Holy shit!

Where did they get a picture of

my mother?"

The reaction I had when I first got a look at my new name tag at Rolling Green.

BARB'S QUIPS

"Don't wear a thong
with your Depends."

More advice for us oldies: Don't wear a nose ring with
your bifocals or compression socks with short shorts.

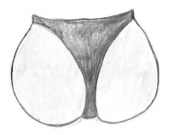

BARB'S QUIPS

"$20!"

"That's $50!"

"Just give me your credit card!"

Bruce likes to sneak a peek when my caregiver is giving me a shower in the morning. But it costs him!

After years as North Carolinians, Bruce and I are planning to stay in Greenville, SC at the continuing care facility where we are actively trying to build new friendships. I'm becoming accustomed to the new caregivers I'll need to help me through the rest of life's journey. My days still require cycles of therapy and continue to test my inner strength and willingness to lean on others.

What we did not anticipate was the diminished contact with family members and close friends. I liken it to when someone dies, and it is hard for folks to know what to say. I know they are with us in spirit and would come if we asked. But it is also hard to ask. So, if you are reading this, just phone or video call me.

Letting go of independence has and will continue to be the biggest challenge in my journey. This is where Bruce has been my hero and my rock. I pray that all the Pearls in my life will also continue to be there for me, with an extra bit of love and care.

My advice; never give up on old friends. Each phase of life and the friends you make should be nurtured and held onto. Keep your team large. There are no limits on the number of people who fit in your life. Some groups have begun to overlap...and now help each other. The circle grows!

We have endeavored to name all the friends who have been there for us since my ordeal began, at the risk of leaving someone out. As you see on the following page, there are so many of you who stepped up, pitched in, rallied forth, and circled the wagons!

We love you all.

With Love,
Barb

Dedicated To All The Pearls In Our Life

BOB & AMOR / FERN / CYNTHIA & DICK / LINDA & STEPHEN / ANN & BOB / JOYCE & JOHN / DEBBIE & JOHN / MARY ANN / MARY & DAVE / TOM & DOT / HOLLY, BEN & KIDS / COLIN, KATE & KIDS / ANN K / BRENDA / POLLY / MARION & MARSHALL / DEBBIE & HEINZ / LINDA & BRYAN / LYNDA & TOM / MARY & JOHN / DAWN & TIM / KAREN & RON / JORDAN & DYLAN / STEPHANIE & SHANE / SUSAN & STEVE / MOLLOY / CATHY & JIM / REBECCA & BRANDON / HERSCHEL & NANCY / JUNE & DAN / SANDRA & LARRY / "G","T" & SHIRLEY / KRIS & KIP / JOYCE & LEN / PAT & LARRY / JILL & PETE / SKYLAR, J.D. & J.T / COURTNEY & MAITLAND / MEG / TOM B / THE PEARLIE GIRLS / M.T. & SUE / NARIAN & DAVE / JANET & WAYNE / KATHY & TRACEY / CHRIS & JIM / GINO & FAMILY / KELLY V / GLENDA & ANN R / BARB & MIKE / CINDY D / DIANE D / DEBBIE & BRUCE & ALYSSA / TERRY & JOHN / SUSAN & DAVE / RUTH W / CHARLES B / JESSICA & DR. MATT / RGV THERAPY / DR. SCOTT L / ALISON, KELLY & CINDY / DR. COOK & NANCY / REV. MARK / CONNIE (PINES) / AMANDA, TREVOR, ASHLEY & GAVIN

SIGNS OF A STROKE

Stroke is the fifth cause of death and a leading cause of severe, long-term disability in the U.S., according to The American Stroke Association, a division of the American Heart Association.

Strokes can happen to anyone – any age, any time.

Use the letters BE FAST to spot a stroke:

BALANCE:
Trouble walking, dizziness, loss of balance, or lack of coordination

EYESIGHT:
Double vision or loss of vision in one or both eyes

FACE:
Facial drooping, typically on one side or the other

ARMS:
Sudden numbness or weakness in the arm, face, or leg, especially on one side of the body

SPEECH:
Slurred speech, inability to speak, or difficulty understanding speech

TIME:
Time is critical if experiencing these symptoms. Seek help immediately. Call 911 right away.

Anterior Circulation Stroke occurs when blood vessels in the front part of the brain are blocked. Symptoms may include:

- Sudden NUMBNESS or weakness of the face, arm, or leg, especially on one side of the body
- Sudden CONFUSION, trouble speaking or understanding speech
- Sudden TROUBLE SEEING in one or both eyes
- Sudden TROUBLE WALKING, dizziness, loss of balance or coordination
- Sudden SEVERE HEADACHE with no known cause

Posterior Circulation Stroke occurs when blood vessels in the back part of the brain are blocked. Symptoms can be very different than anterior (front) circulation strokes. Symptoms include:

- Vertigo, like the room is spinning
- Imbalance
- One-sided arm or leg weakness
- Slurred speech or dysarthria
- Double vision or other vision problems
- A headache
- Nausea and/or vomiting

Know Your Risk

According to the CDC, nearly 50% of all adult men and 44% of women have high blood pressure, and a higher risk for stroke. High blood pressure is more common in non-Hispanic black adults (56%) than in non-Hispanic white adults (48%), non-Hispanic Asian adults (46%), or Hispanic adults (39%).

Blood Pressure Categories

American Heart Association.

BLOOD PRESSURE CATEGORY	SYSTOLIC mm Hg (upper number)		DIASTOLIC mm Hg (lower number)
NORMAL	LESS THAN 120	and	LESS THAN 80
ELEVATED	120-129	and	LESS THAN 80
HIGH BLOOD PRESSURE (HYPERTENSION) STAGE 1	130-139	or	80-89
HIGH BLOOD PRESSURE (HYPERTENSION) STAGE 2	140 OR HIGHER	or	90 OR HIGHER
HYPERTENSIVE CRISIS (consult your doctor immediately)	HIGHER THAN 180	and/or	HIGHER THAN 120

heart.org/bplevels

If you suspect you or someone is experiencing a stroke

CALL 911
IMMEDIATELY

It is also critical to have your cholesterol checked at least every 5 years or more often if you have contributing conditions.

Myths: All cholesterol is bad for you. I would be able to feel it if I had high cholesterol.

- **LDL (low-density lipoprotein), sometimes called "bad" cholesterol,** makes up most of your body's cholesterol. High levels of LDL cholesterol raise your risk for heart disease and stroke.

- **HDL (high-density lipoprotein), or "good" cholesterol,** carries cholesterol back to the liver. The liver then flushes it from the body. So high levels of HDL cholesterol can lower your risk for heart disease and stroke.

PREVENTING A STROKE

According to the CDC, up to 80% of strokes can be prevented through healthy lifestyle changes and controlling health conditions that raise your risk for stroke.

Having high cholesterol or high blood pressure increases stroke risk, as does being overweight. Here's what you can do:

– Eat a healthy diet with lots of fresh fruits and vegetables.

– Eat foods low in saturated fats, trans fat, and cholesterol but high in fiber, which can help curb high cholesterol levels.

– Limit salt intake to maintain healthy blood pressure.

– Exercise to maintain a healthy weight and lower both cholesterol and blood pressure levels.

– Other lifestyle factors, such as quitting smoking, can also lower the risk of stroke.

Older age and family history of strokes are among the things that make you more likely to have a stroke. Unfortunately, you can't turn back the clock or change your relatives.

1 in 4 stroke survivors will have another stroke.

It's okay to start small, but don't give up. The good news is it's not just for preventing stroke but preventing dementia as well, according to Dr. Cheryl Bushnell, a neurologist, and director of the Comprehensive Stroke Center at Wake Forest Baptist Health in Winston-Salem, North Carolina.

Start a conversation with your doctor on this topic. Don't wait for them to ask. Preventing a stroke is something you can take control over.

Here are some ways to get started on the road to prevention:

If you smoke, quit
For every five cigarettes a person smokes each day, the risk of having a stroke goes up by 12%. For Black adults, smoking cigarettes more than doubles the risk of stroke.

Move more
More active men and women have a 25%-30% lower risk of stroke than those least active. Even moving around for 10 minutes every hour is better than sitting for an extended period. Set the alarm! 30 minutes of active exercise per day is ideal.

Keep blood pressure under control
While it can be controlled through lifestyle changes or medication, only about 1 in 5 adults keep it properly managed. Use at-home monitoring and regular communication with doctors to ensure medications are working.

Keep cholesterol under control
Everyone over 20 should get their cholesterol levels tested at least every five years. Like blood pressure, it can be managed through lifestyle changes or by taking medication, but regular monitoring and communication with doctors are needed.

Eat better foods
A healthy weight is important, but nutrition is more important than weight loss. Eat fruits, vegetables, low-fat dairy, whole grains, fish, and nuts, while cutting back on foods high in saturated fats, cholesterol, and trans fats.

Cut the booze
Too much alcohol can raise your blood pressure and triglycerides. Limit yourself to no more than two drinks a day if you're a man and one drink if you are a woman. That's 12 oz. of beer, 5 oz. of wine, or 1.2 oz of distilled spirits.

Control diabetes
If your doctor thinks you have symptoms of diabetes, they may recommend that you get tested. If you have diabetes, check your blood sugar levels regularly and talk with your health care team about treatment options.

Treat heart disease

If you have certain heart conditions, such as coronary artery disease or atrial fibrillation (irregular heartbeat), your health care team may recommend medical treatment or surgery. Taking care of heart problems can help prevent stroke.

Take your medicine
Follow your doctor's instructions carefully, if you take medicine to treat heart disease, high cholesterol, high blood pressure, or diabetes. Always ask questions if you don't understand something. Never stop taking your medicine without first talking to your doctor or pharmacist.

Work with your health care team
You and your health care team can work together to prevent or treat the medical conditions that lead to stroke. Discuss your treatment plan regularly and bring a list of questions to your appointments. Learn how to find the right doctor for you.

If you've already had a stroke, your health care team will work with you to prevent further strokes. Your treatment plan will include medicine or surgery and lifestyle changes to lower your risk for another stroke. Be sure to take your medicine as directed and follow your doctor's instructions.

Start early
Strokes happen to young people, too. About 10%-15% of all strokes occur in adults aged 50 or under. Recent research shows Black young adults have up to four times the risk of their white peers.

IF YOU HAVE A STROKE

Seconds count in stroke care. Artificial intelligence speeds up stroke care in rural areas.

Every four minutes, someone in the U.S. dies of a stroke. It's one of the most common neurological diseases and a leading cause of disability, said Dr. James S. McKinney III, a neurologist and medical director of the Neuroscience Institute at Novant Health New Hanover Regional Medical Center in Wilmington, North Carolina.

Every minute a stroke is left untreated can mean the difference between permanent disability and a full recovery. That's because up to 2 million brain cells die every 60 seconds when oxygen and nutrients are cut off.

To speed treatment, Novant Health partnered with Viz.ai, a software platform that uses artificial intelligence to synchronize stroke care and reduce delays that can stand between patients and lifesaving treatments. Every Novant Health stroke specialist has access to Viz.ai on their smartphone.

In a rural hospital setting, it often takes at least an hour to get results from some of the more critical scans. Viz.ai sends the scan immediately to the 'cloud' to be read by artificial intelligence.

The technology analyzes images for a suspected blockage of one of the main arteries of the brain, known as a large vessel occlusion stroke (or LVO stroke). This saves time and brain cells.

"This is about leveraging technology," McKinney said. "By using this, we can extend ourselves out into the rural communities. People have immediate access to neurovascular expertise, right at the push of a button."

If you suspect you or someone is experiencing a stroke

CALL 911
IMMEDIATELY

American Stroke Association
www.stroke.org
Stroke Family Warmline:
1-888-4-STROKE or 1-888-478-7653
Monday-Friday: 8AM-5PM CST

Centers for Disease Control and Prevention (CDC)
www.cdc.gov/stroke
800-232-4636

"My Stroke of Insight: A Brain Scientist's Personal Journey"
by Jill Bolte Taylor, Ph.D.
www.mystrokeofinsight.com

Novant Health Neurology
Dr. James S. McKinney III
Wilmington, NC
910-662-7500

Barb Kwaiser

Barb Kwaiser lives in Greenville, SC with Bruce, her husband of 60 years and book contributor, and near their daughter and book illustrator Kris Wynne. An avid lifelong reader, Barb never expected to author a book, but the experience of suffering a massive stroke taught her so many life lessons she was eager to share with her "Pearls" and others facing the same adversity.

Co-author, Linda Worrell, lives in Lake Wylie, SC and met Barb in their book club, The Pearlie Girls. Recently retired from a career in marketing and business consulting, Linda is pleased to be putting her journalism degree to new use. This is her first publication, thanks to the partnership and tenacity of her dear friends Barb and Bruce. Linda can be reached at linda_worrell@att.net.

NOTES

Made in United States
North Haven, CT
15 July 2022

21323502R00059